STOURBRIDGE
TO
WOLVERHAMPTON

Vic Mitchell and Keith Smith

MP Middleton Press

Front cover: Pictured under the long-forgotten roof at Wolverhampton Low Level is class 3232, a single framed 2-4-0 no. 3234. (P.Q.Treloar coll.)

Back cover: Standing outside its shed near the bay platform at Stourbridge Junction in 2006 is a Parry People Mover. Flywheel power proved ideal for the Stourbridge Town branch. (G.Sidwell)

Published December 2007

ISBN 978 1 906008 16 1

© Middleton Press, 2007

Design Deborah Esher
Typesetting Barbara Mitchell

Published by
> *Middleton Press*
> *Easebourne Lane*
> *Midhurst*
> *West Sussex*
> *GU29 9AZ*

Tel: 01730 813169
Fax: 01730 812601
Email: info@middletonpress.co.uk
www.middletonpress.co.uk

Printed & bound by Biddles Ltd, Kings Lynn

INDEX

ACKNOWLEDGEMENTS

We are very grateful for the assistance received from many of those mentioned in the credits also to A.R.Carder, L.Crosier, G.Croughton, S.C.Jenkins, N.Langridge, B.Lewis, J.W.Mann, Mr D. and Dr S.Salter, N.Williams, E.Wilmshurst and in particular, our always supportive wives, Barbara Mitchell and Janet Smith.

I. Railway Clearing House map of 1947.

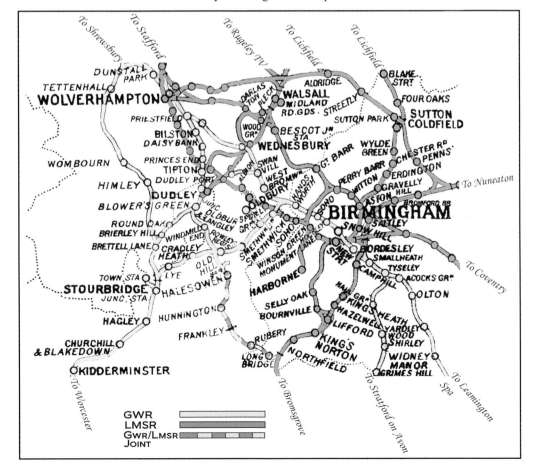

GEOGRAPHICAL SETTING

The route traversed the western part of the Black Country, so called on account of the smoke and dirt resulting from the working of local deposits of coal and iron, particularly during the 19th century. An extensive canal network had been established in the early part of this period, although the area is a high plateau with few natural watercourses.

There is a notable ridge in the vicinity of Dudley, which divides the area and gave rise to a castle. There were thus steep gradients and a lengthy tunnel. A multitude of industries, both heavy and light, covered the area of the lines, except for the Halesowen-Rubery section, which is outside the Black Country. Manufactured products ranged from glass at Stourbridge to cars at Longbridge.

The maps are to the scale of 6 ins to 1 mile, with north at the top, unless otherwise indicated. The gradient profiles for the main line are near caption nos 2, 82 and 113, while those for the branch are near nos 28, X and 53. However, the gradients changed many times, due to mining subsidence.

HISTORICAL BACKGROUND

The Oxford, Worcester & Wolverhampton Railway reached Stourbridge on 2nd May 1852 and it was extended to Dudley on 20th December of that year. The branch from it to Stourbridge Basin did not open until 1859 and the branch to Stourbridge Town came into use in 1879.

The Dudley-Wolverhampton section followed on 1st December 1853. Almost the entire route from Oxford had a third rail for broad gauge trains, but this was never used regularly and was lifted in 1858. The OWWR became part of the West Midland Railway in 1860 and this was absorbed by the Great Western Railway in 1863.

At Wolverhampton and Tipton connections were made with the 1852 Birmingham, Wolverhampton & Stour Valley Railway (London & North Western Railway from 1867). North of Wolverhampton, a link was made with the former Grand Junction Railway to Stafford (LNWR from 1846).

Dudley had been reached from the east by the South Staffordshire Railway in 1850, this becoming part of the LNWR in 1867. A branch from Stourbridge Junction to Cradley opened in 1863 and this was eventually extended to Birmingham, becoming GWR property.

A branch south from Dudley to Halesowen was opened by the GWR on 1st March 1878. This was extended south to Longbridge on the Midland Railway's Birmingham & Gloucester line of 1840 on 1st November 1883. Known as the Halesowen Railway, it became a MR/GWR Joint line in 1906 and passenger service was withdrawn in 1919.

North of Brettell Lane was a goods branch opened by the OWWR to Bromley Basin in 1858. In 1925, most of this became part of a new passenger line to Wolverhampton, via Wombourn, but the service was withdrawn in 1932.

The Old Hill-Halesowen passenger service was withdrawn on 3rd December 1927, but trains for workmen at the car factory were provided between 31st March 1928 and 1st September 1958.

The GWR became the Western Region of British Railways upon nationalisation in 1948. The route was transferred to the London Midland Region in June 1964.

Other passenger closures followed thus: Stourbridge Junction-Wolverhampton (except Priestfield) on 30th July 1962 and Old Hill-Dudley on 15th June 1964. Details of closures to freight traffic are given in the captions, but the creation of the Dudley Freightliner Terminal in 1967 should be mentioned here, as should the closure of the route south of Dudley to through goods traffic in 1993. The northern part had been lost in 1968.

PASSENGER SERVICES

Main Line

The first London-Wolverhampton service over the route was of four weekdays trains, these using the LNWR stations at both ends of their journey. By 1857, there were nine trains between Stourbridge and Wolverhampton (Low Level), plus three extra north to Dudley.

The table below indicates departures north from Stourbridge Junction.

	To Dudley only	To Wolverhampton		Sundays Slow
		Fast	Stopping	
1862	1	3	5	?
1870	2	2	9	6
1890	1	5	10	6
1910	2	5	14	10
1930	5	3	17	5
1950	6	0	13	5
1962	2	2	7	5

Trains from London diminished after 1910, probably due to the opening of the direct route via Bicester. The remaining fast trains were mostly from Hereford or beyond, some being destined for Manchester. After 1921, express trains were redesignated semi-fast on this route. By 1951, there were only two lethargic weekday trains from London, with one on Sundays, even slower. These lasted only a few years.

Dudley-Halesowen

The frequency of southbound trains is given below:

	Dudley-Old Hill		Old Hill-Halesowen	
	Weekdays	Sundays	Weekdays	Sundays
July 1878	10	4	10	5
February 1890	10	0	14	0
July 1905	24	5	13	6
July 1910	20	5	26	9

Sunday trains were withdrawn in 1915, owing to the demands of World War I. The weekday service to Halesowen until withdrawal in 1927 usually comprised 25 trips.

The trains through Windmill End in most of the 1940s and 1950s usually numbered about 24. The final timetable revision began on 9th June 1958 and comprised eight trips on Mondays to Fridays (in the peak hours) and just two on Saturdays.

Halesowen southwards

The initial service comprised four MR trains to Northfield and three of GWR stock running only to Rubery. We have found no evidence of Sunday trains on this section. The GWR trains were withdrawn in October 1886, but the MR continued to run four. By 1905 it was five trains, usually to Kings Norton, these running until January 1917, when the service was reduced to one. This seems to have ceased in 1919; the workers trains remained unpublicised.

II.   The 1901 edition has the route to Wolverhampton at the top and the line to Old Hill and Birmingham on the right. Top left is the canal basin and earthworks of the original rope-worked 1 in 14 branch of 1859. Part of the track remains, close to the engine shed.

III. The 1921 survey shows the position of the junction and its station since 1st October 1901. Town station remained in the same place (top left), but its double track was single from March 1935. At the top is Stambermill Viaduct, which was originally one of Brunel's timber designs. It was rebuilt in 1882. The siding to Stepping Stones Works was in use until 1949.

1. There is sparse visual record of the first station. Thus we only offer this view of the up (east side) building. The entrance to the goods yard was behind it and a siding was laid on its site after 1901. (Lens of Sutton coll.)

2. The north end of the 1901 four-platformed station is seen in the 1920s as 4-4-0 no. 3444 *Cormorant* runs past Middle Box. The locomotive was in use from 1909 to 1951. The box housed a panel from August 1990. (LCGB/P.Q.Treloar coll.)

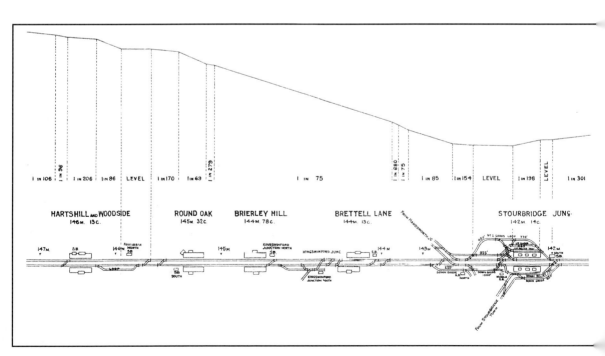

3.   This view in the other direction from almost the same location is of 0-6-0PT no. 7402 shunting South Yard on 24th March 1951. Attached to it is a GWR style shunters truck. (B.W.L.Brooksbank)

4.   From the same favoured location on the same day we can enjoy 4-6-0 no. 6936 *Breccles Hall* passing Middle Box with a Birmingham Snow Hill to Hereford train. The Stourbridge Town branch is in the left background. (B.W.L.Brooksbank)

5.   The Stourbridge Town Shuttle ("The Dodger") was being worked by 0-4-2T no. 1414 on 10th September 1955. One autocoach sufficed until the introduction of DMUs. The entrance building (right) was replaced by the present small ticket office in 1997. The ringed signals were for goods trains. (N.Stead/M.J.Stretton coll.)

6.   The photographer was standing opposite Middle Box in February 1966 to record the four well protected platforms. The three tracks on the left were carriage sidings and to their right are two goods lines. Both island platforms had once featured refreshment rooms. (R.G.Nelson/T.Walsh)

Our *Worcester to Birmingham* album contains other views of this station and also of Stourbridge Town together with the canal basin goods yard beyond it.

7.   The canopies were greatly reduced in length and reclad in about 1977. The result is seen in June 1990, as a DMU waits to run down the steep gradient to Stourbridge Town. The platform had become a bay in 1971 and the corresponding track on the east side, together with the parallel sidings, had given way to car park spaces. (D.A.Thompson)

8.   South Box closed in 1973, North Box in 1978, leaving only the former Middle Box to be photographed on 23rd July 2006. It is seen from the Parry People Mover, which operated the Sunday branch service for most of that year. It is illustrated on the back cover. Beyond the box and bush are the six sidings of the 2004 Chiltern Railways Depot. (V.Mitchell)

9.   The engine sheds were more than one mile north of Stourbridge Junction station. The first one was completed in 1870 and had four roads; these buildings were a little to the north and were completed in 1926. The ash pit area was clean and tidy when photographed on 10th November 1963. There was a central 65ft turntable from which 28 tracks radiated. (R.S.Carpenter)

10.   BR erected a shed nearby and it became a diesel depot in 1956. It was recorded in April 1962 when it housed about 12 class 08 diesels. Steam ceased at the depot in July 1966. (R.S.Carpenter)

11.   Stourbridge Engine Shed box is pictured in November 1963. It was immediately north of the 190yd long Stambermill, Amblecote or Stourbridge Viaduct and was closed on 11th May 1969. It had a new 33-lever frame in 1912. (R.S.Carpenter)

BRETTELL LANE

IVa. Our route is from lower left to top right, the diverging line running to Wombourn. Close study of this 1901 edition will reveal the extensive working of iron, coal and clay at that time, the GWR benefitting accordingly. This station is lower left, while the next one is top right. The divergence is at Kingswinford Junction, the line on the left running to Bromley Barn from 1858.

Inset is the 1884 edition at 25 ins to 1 mile.

12.   A southward panorama from the main road in 1955 includes the signal box, which was destroyed by fire in 1961. It had a 31-lever frame. (Stations UK)

13.   Looking under the main road on 12th October 1961, we see the bridge carrying Bull Street. The goods yard remained open until 5th July 1965. All facilities had been extended in 1897. (R.G.Nelson/T.Walsh)

14.   A southward view on the same day includes the crane, which was rated at 12 tons. Parcel traffic increased from 28,000 in 1913 to 46,000 in 1936. (R.G.Nelson/T.Walsh)

15.   There was a staff of 34 to 40 in the 1930s, but there was no-one to clear the weeds in the final years. Note that gas lighting remained to the end. Parcel traffic was handled to the end of 1966. (Lens of Sutton coll.)

BRIERLEY HILL

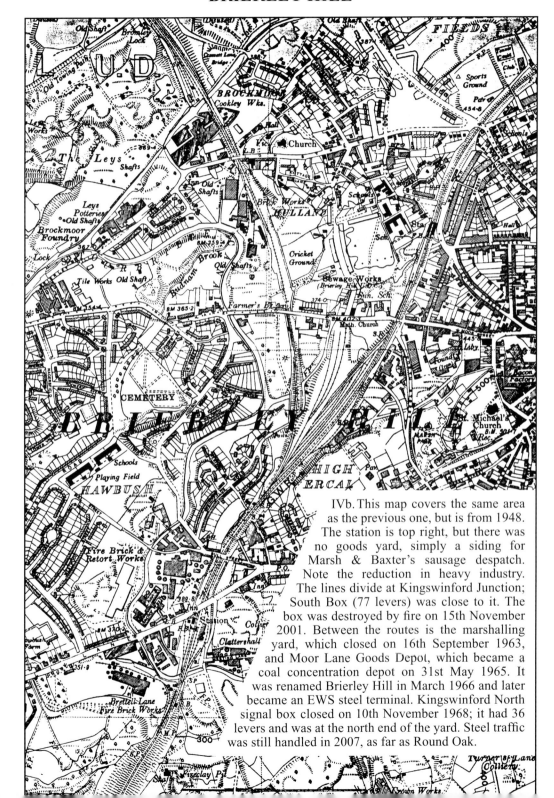

IVb. This map covers the same area as the previous one, but is from 1948. The station is top right, but there was no goods yard, simply a siding for Marsh & Baxter's sausage despatch. Note the reduction in heavy industry. The lines divide at Kingswinford Junction; South Box (77 levers) was close to it. The box was destroyed by fire on 15th November 2001. Between the routes is the marshalling yard, which closed on 16th September 1963, and Moor Lane Goods Depot, which became a coal concentration depot on 31st May 1965. It was renamed Brierley Hill in March 1966 and later became an EWS steel terminal. Kingswinford North signal box closed on 10th November 1968; it had 36 levers and was at the north end of the yard. Steel traffic was still handled in 2007, as far as Round Oak.

16.   The station opened after the others, on 1st December 1858. This is a view north in 1958. Twenty years earlier, there had been a staff of nine here. (Stations UK)

17.   The wide space between the tracks is a relic of broad gauge days, although the station was built at about the time of the removal of the outer rail. The photograph is from October 1961. (R.G.Nelson/T.Walsh)

18.   No. 4179 is southbound, not long before the withdrawal of passenger service. There had been over 1500 season tickets issued in 1929, but only 378 ten years later. Parcel traffic continued until the end of 1966. (Stephenson Locomotive Society coll.)

19.   Rochester pattern Suggs gas lights were in use to the end. As light industry grew, so did parcel traffic: 33,000 in 1913 to 115,000 in 1938. The nearby steel terminal at Moor Lane was in use until 2nd May 1997. (Lens of Sutton coll.)

ROUND OAK

Fens Pool
(Canal Feeder)

Woodside

Woodside Park

Harts Hill &
Woodside Sta.

Woodside Colliery
Clay Pit (Pit No. 1)

Parkhead Colliery
(Pit No. 2)
(Disused)

Blowers
Lock

Old Coal
Shaft

HART'S
HILL

Glass
Works

Woodside
Iron Works

Old Coal
Shaft

Old
Limekiln

Peartreelane
Bridge

Woodside Colliery
(Pit No. 14)
(Disused)

Tramway
Depot

Colliery
(Dis.)

Brierleyhill
Iron Wks.

Woodside Br.
The
Hurst

Hurst Works

Old Coal Shafts

ROUND
OAK

BCN
CANAL

Towing Path

DUDLEY CANAL

Round Oak Wks.
(Iron & Steel)

Old Coal Shafts

Old Level
Colliery
(Disused)

Hurst
Colliery

TWO LOCKS LINE

Lower
Hurst

Level New
Furnaces

Gas Wks.
(Disused)

Saltwells Colliery
(Disused)

Grange

Picture Ho.

Football
Gd.

Market

Old Shaft
Colliery
(Disused)

Old
Shafts

Old Level
Iron Works

Pit No. 14
(Disused)

Incline

Saltwells Colliery

Saltwells Colliery
Pit No. 36
(Disused)

Saltwells
House

**BRIERLEY
HILL**

Saltwells Colliery
(Pit No. 29)
(Disused)

Ninelocks
Wharf

Ninelocks Works

Ninelocks
Bridge

Old Coal
Shafts

Saltwells Colliery
(Pit No. 28)
(Disused)

TRAMWAY

Coal
Level

Tinsyford
Bridge

New
Robin Hood
Colliery
Pit No. 36

Coal
Shafts

MINERAL RAILWAY

Saltwells W

Saltwells Inn

Salt Wells

Infectious

Lodge F

Do

V.   The left of this map borders onto
the two previous ones, but it is from 1921.
The station is on the left; the one shown top
right had closed in 1917. Note the numerous
canals and the Earl of Dudley's Railway
crossing the GWR. Woodside Branch is
above centre and terminates at Woodside
Bridge. There were seven different signal
boxes carrying the name "Round Oak" over
the years and there was one at Harts Hill &
Woodside until 1928.

20.   Southbound is 2-6-2T no. 4161 with local compartment stock, but the end is nigh judging by the weeds. The staff had numbered 23 in 1923, but it was down to 17 in 1933.
(Stephenson Locomotive Society coll.)

21.   Industry is both sides of the line in this view southwest in 1961. Freight despatched in 1913 included 86,000 tons of general merchandise and 111,000 tons of minerals, excluding coal. Most of the coal produced locally was used locally, only 5000 tons going away by rail that year.
(R.G.Nelson/T.Walsh)

Earl of Dudley's Railways

Just north of Rouns Oak, the GWR crossed over the EODR on the level. The EODR comprised the Kingswinford Railway (or Shut End Railway) and the Pensnett Railway. The Shut End section opened, with steam traction, on 2nd June 1829, but the extensive system was not connected to the national network until 1865, outbound traffic having gone by canal. The Pensnett section opened in 1846, again with steam traction. The zenith of the Earl's lines was the 1870-90 period, with 40 miles of track needing 152 employees and 11 locos at one period, but local iron sources were becoming exhausted. Mileage was greatly reduced by the 1950s and dieselisation took place in 1963. The end of the remnants came with the closure of Round Oak Steelworks in 1982.

22.   This is a 1908 view of the Earl of Dudley's Railway's sidings at The Wallows, seen top left of map V. Before the opening of Baggeridge Junction in 1925, coal from the Earl's collieries at Himley and Baggeridge was brought here for both despatch on the GWR and for internal use in the Round Oak Steelworks. (G.M.Perkins/R.S.Carpenter coll.)

23.   Ashwood Basin was on the Staffordshire & Worcestershire Canal and was the western terminus of the Earl of Dudley's Railway system, dating back to its opening in 1829. Today it is a marina for pleasure craft and virtually all signs of the railway tracks on both sides of the basin have disappeared. (G.M.Perkins/R.S.Carpenter coll.)

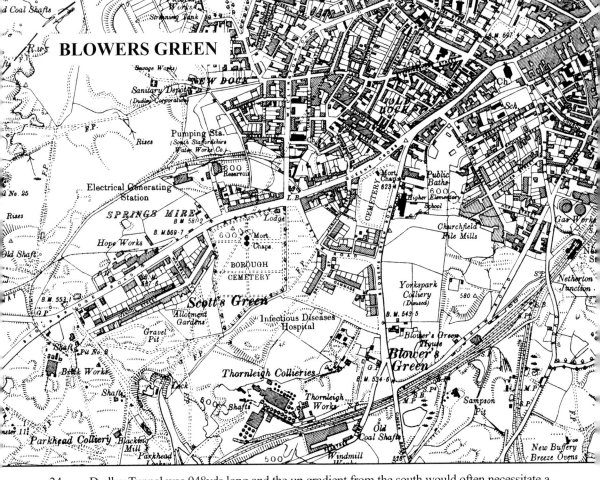

BLOWERS GREEN

24.   Dudley Tunnel was 948yds long and the up gradient from the south would often necessitate a banking engine. They would draw away from the train as it entered the tunnel and then reverse over the crossover at the far end of the platforms. The station closed to passengers on 30th July 1962, although Dudley-Old Hill trains passed through for another two years. (P.J.Garland/R.S.Carpenter coll.)

← VI. Netherton station (right) was renamed Blowers Green in 1921, the year in which this map was published. The original Netherton station closed in 1878, when the branch (lower right) opened to Halesowen. Dudley Tunnel begins on the right of the map. The station was called Dudley South Side for a period between the other names.

25. Bound for Dudley on 30th June 1959 is 0-6-0PT no. 6418 with a parcels van. The line to Old Hill and Halesowen curves to the left and was in use for freight until 1st January 1968. The signal box was in use until 30th March 1969 and had 31 levers. (P.J.Garland/R.S.Carpenter coll.)

26. A northward view from the bridge in the previous picture in October 1962 shows the platforms in the final year of use. The signal arm on the right is for branch trains. Dudley gasworks dominates the area. (R.G.Nelson/T.Walsh)

Windmill End Branch

SOUTH OF BLOWERS GREEN

27.   This northward view is from the bridge lower right on the previous map (VI) and features a Dudley-Old Hill service in about 1963. On the left is part of the South Staffs Wagon Repair Works. (D.Wilson)

Great Western Railway.
BRIERLEY HILL
TO
HARTLEBURY
THIRD CLASS
Issued as per Company's Time Bills
SEP 8 68   279

Gt Western Ry   Gt Western Ry
Round Oak   Round Oak
TO
DUDLEY
via Windmill End
THIRD CLASS
4d   Fare   4d
Issued subject to the conditions & regulations set out in the Company's Time Tables Bills & Notices
DUDLEY   DUDLEY
5875   5875

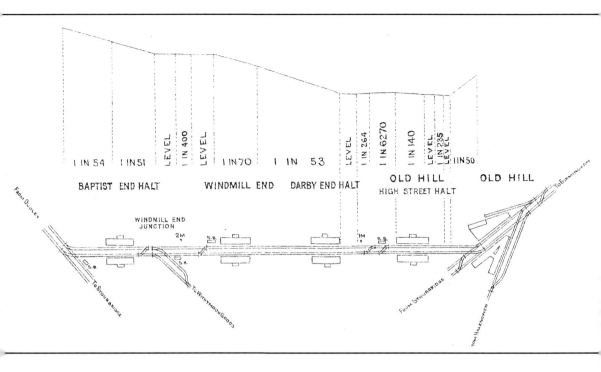

I IN 54   I IN 51   LEVEL   I IN 400   LEVEL   I IN 70   I IN 53   LEVEL   I IN 264   I IN 6270   I IN 140   LEVEL   I IN 235   LEVEL   I IN 50

BAPTIST END HALT   WINDMILL END   DARBY END HALT   OLD HILL HIGH STREET HALT   OLD HILL

WINDMILL END JUNCTION

FROM DUDLEY — TO STOURBRIDGE — TO WITHYMOOR GOODS — FROM STOURBRIDGE — FROM HALESOWEN — TO BIRMINGHAM

28.   Northbound and about to pass under the same bridge on 29th April 1963 is a railcar from Old Hill. It is on the curve at the top of the next map and Baptist End Halt is in the distance. Most local services in the area were operated by DMUs from 17th June 1957. (D.Wilson)

BAPTIST END HALT

VII.   This map continues south from the previous one and is also from 1921. On the right are the stops at Windmill End and Darby End. In the centre is the Withymoor Basin Branch, which opened on 10th May 1879 and closed on 5th July 1965. The basin was renamed Netherton on 1st August 1921, for railway purposes. To the right of the branch are Bumble Hole Ballast Sidings.

29.   The halt opened on 21st August 1905 and was initially served by steam railmotors. The original structure is seen on 28th May 1956 as ex-GWR diesel railcar no. W14 calls on its way to Old Hill. (T.J.Edgington)

30.   The rebuilt platforms and new shelters are seen in 1958. The locality was noted for hand forged tubes. (Stations UK)

31.   A Pannier tank and autocoach arrive from Old Hill sometime in 1963, having just run past Windmill End Junction signal box. There is evidence on both sides of the train of the descending footpaths. (D.Wilson)

SOUTH OF BAPTIST END HALT

32.   A closer view of Windmill End Junction in 1963 includes the unusual sight of a railcar coming off the goods-only branch to Netherton Basin. The box closed on 5th July 1965; it had a 30-lever frame. (D.Wilson)

WINDMILL END

33.   No. 3778 is propelling the 6.24pm Dudley to Old Hill on 30th July 1955, although the locomotive was not fitted for push-pull working. A competent crew could break the rules safely. (Stephenson Locomotive Society coll.)

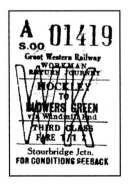

34. The station was downgraded to a halt in 1952 and became unstaffed. This is the grim sight of the west side, shortly before demolition in 1955-56. Parcels despatched had included forks, spades, sinks and homing pigeons. (P.Coutanche coll.)

35. Parts lie everywhere as a train leaves for Dudley on 15th September 1956. The lamp is remote from the arm as it is a fixed distant, which means a permanent caution. (H.C.Casserley)

36.   Ex-GWR railcar no. W8 is working the 5.36pm Old Hill to Dudley on 20th August 1957 and is waiting near the temporary building. The gas lights remain globeless. (T.J.Edgington)

37.   By 1958, the platforms and shelters were complete, but no lights were provided. Vandal proof ones were not then easily available. The exposed location had been ideal for a windmill. (Stations UK)

DARBY END HALT

38.   The halt is lower right on the last map and it came into use with the others on the branch on 21st August 1905. The remains are seen from a train from Dudley on 13th August 1955. (R.M.Casserley)

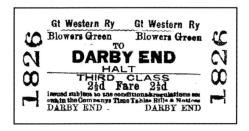

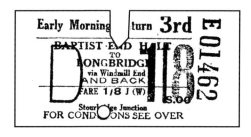

39.   Entirely new facilities were provided, although basic, and they were recorded in 1958. Again, no illumination was provided, but society was not then litigation mad. Three were eventually erected each side. (Stations UK)

40.   The shelters of the halt are in the centre of this panorama from the north from 1963. Like other pictures, this shows well how past industrial activity had scarred the landscape so extensively. (R.G.Nelson/T.Walsh)

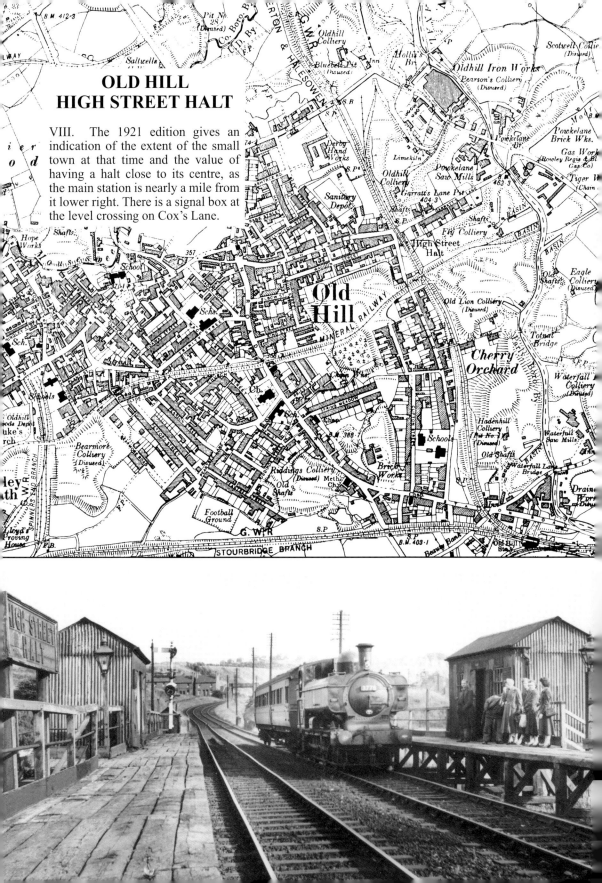

OLD HILL
HIGH STREET HALT

VIII. The 1921 edition gives an indication of the extent of the small town at that time and the value of having a halt close to its centre, as the main station is nearly a mile from it lower right. There is a signal box at the level crossing on Cox's Lane.

41. Northbound is a classic autotrain, headed by 0-6-0PT no. 3778, probably around 1955. The footbridge is at Cherry Orchard. (Stephenson Locomotive Society coll.)

42. Railcar no. W8 is bound for Old Hill on 28th May 1956, having left Dudley at 4.30pm. Concrete components are present ready for the rebuild. (T.J.Edgington)

43. A 1958 picture shows the refurbishment complete and with a lamp post, but no lamp. The distant signal, above the speed limit sign, is also in picture 41, but is too dirty to be seen clearly in that view. (Stations UK)

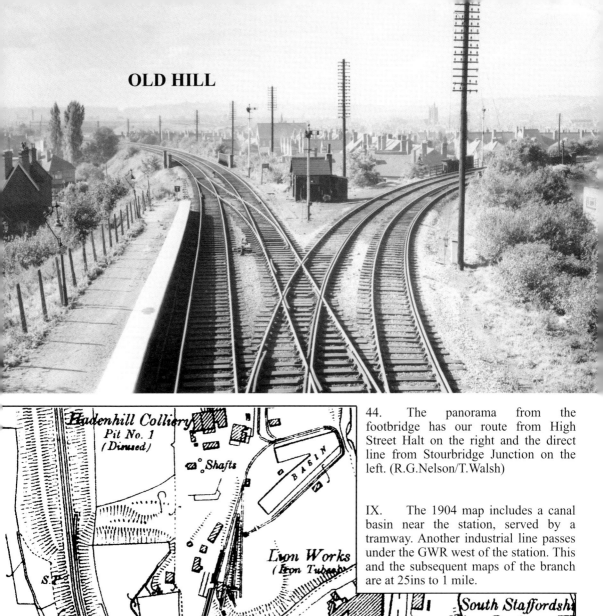

OLD HILL

44. The panorama from the footbridge has our route from High Street Halt on the right and the direct line from Stourbridge Junction on the left. (R.G.Nelson/T.Walsh)

IX. The 1904 map includes a canal basin near the station, served by a tramway. Another industrial line passes under the GWR west of the station. This and the subsequent maps of the branch are at 25ins to 1 mile.

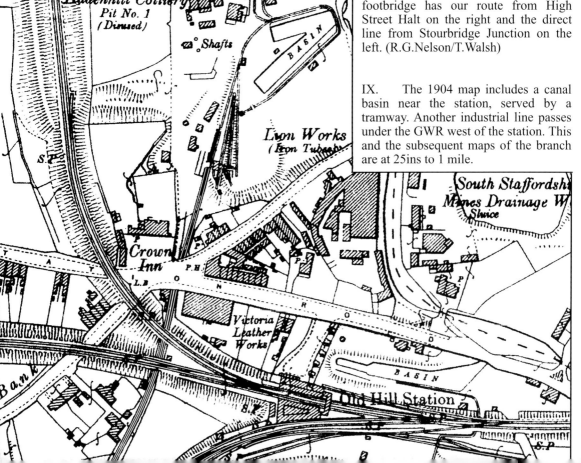

45.   The junction is seen from the Stourbridge platform in 1959; trains for Birmingham use the one on the right. The platform on the left had earlier been served by Halesowen services. (Stations UK)

46.   This is the Halesowen platform in 1959; it had last been used by advertised passenger trains in 1927. The nearest building is the signal box, which was completed in February 1898, 20 years after the north-south route had opened. (Stations UK)

47.   The Halesowen platform was however used by trains for workers at the car factory at Longbridge until 1958. One is arriving on the 1 in 50 up gradient on 8th April 1957, having just passed through Haden Hill Tunnel (151yds long). The lines on the left lasted until 1963. (H.C.Casserley)

48.   The 12.45pm to Dudley awaits departure on a Saturday in 1963. The Halesowen branch signal is in the background. New buildings were opened on 22nd May 1968, following a fire. (D.Wilson)

49.   The signal box spanned the space between the Halesowen and Stourbridge platforms and is seen in 1963. It had 50 levers and was in use until 25th March 1973. (R.G.Nelson/T.Walsh)

Other views of this station can be found in pictures 77 to 81 in our *Worcester to Birmingham* album.

50.   The Halesowen line continued to handle freight until 1968. Beyond it is Palmer's timber yard, which had three sidings until 1963. The station is still open and has modern buildings. (R.G.Nelson/T.Walsh)

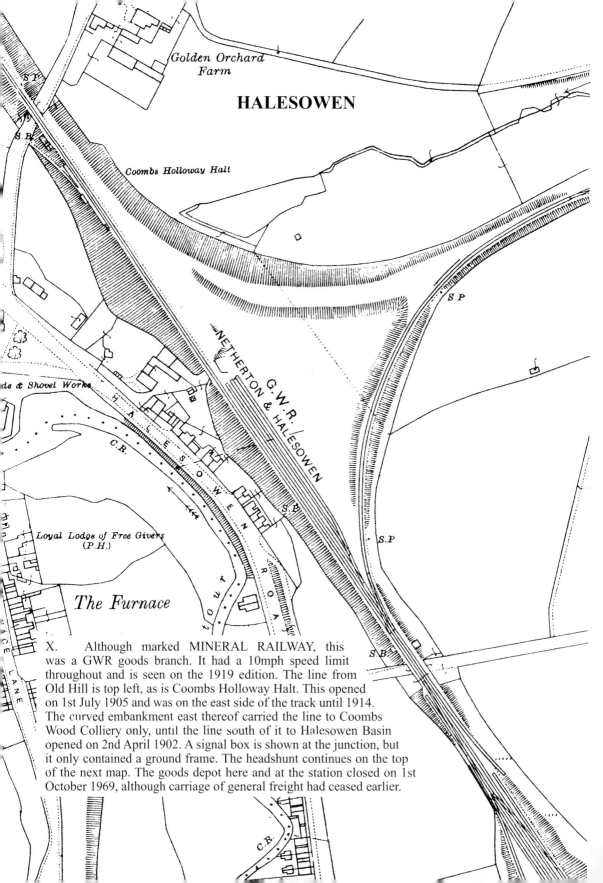

Golden Orchard Farm

HALESOWEN

Coombs Holloway Halt

S.P

S.B.

de & Shovel Works

C.R.

NETHERTON & HALESOWEN

G.W.R.

H A L E S O W E N   R O A D

t o u r

Loyal Lodge of Free Givers
(P.H.)

The Furnace

S.B.

S.P

S.P

S.B.

C.R.

X.   Although marked MINERAL RAILWAY, this
was a GWR goods branch. It had a 10mph speed limit
throughout and is seen on the 1919 edition. The line from
Old Hill is top left, as is Coombs Holloway Halt. This opened
on 1st July 1905 and was on the east side of the track until 1914.
The curved embankment east thereof carried the line to Coombs
Wood Colliery only, until the line south of it to Halesowen Basin
opened on 2nd April 1902. A signal box is shown at the junction, but
it only contained a ground frame. The headshunt continues on the top
of the next map. The goods depot here and at the station closed on 1st
October 1969, although carriage of general freight had ceased earlier.

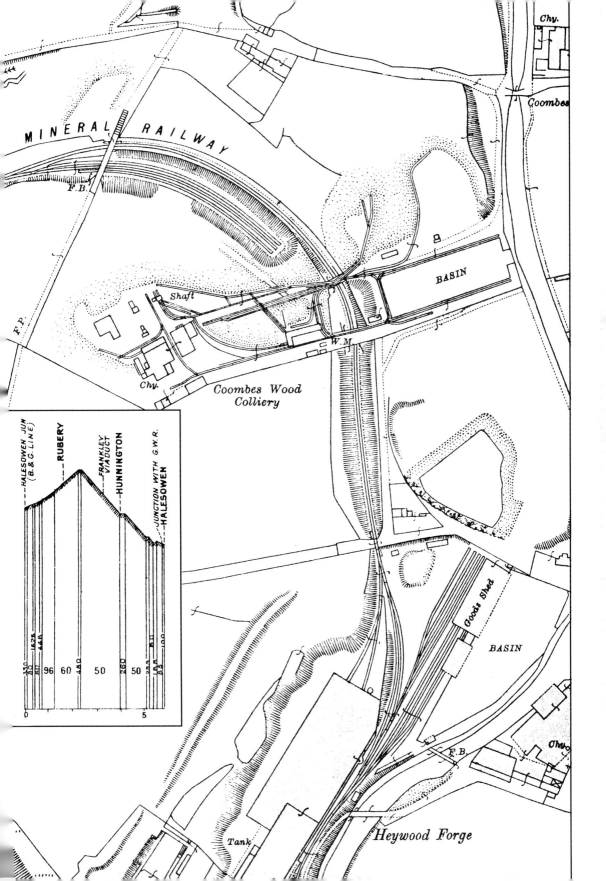

MINERAL RAILWAY

F.B.

F.P.

Shaft

Chy.

W.M.

BASIN

Coombes Wood
Colliery

Chy.

Coombes

HALESOWEN JUN (B.&G. LINE)
RUBERY
FRANKLEY VIADUCT
HUNNINGTON
JUNCTION WITH G.W.R.
HALESOWEN

96   60   450   50   260   50   63

0   5

Goods Shed

BASIN

F.B.

Chy.

Tank

Heywood Forge

51.   The south end of the station was recorded for this postcard, probably in the Edwardian era. The MR services usually originated at Kings Norton, but the working of this station is a mystery. (Lens of Sutton coll.)

52.   This was a frontier station with the MR operating trains south of it and the GWR northwards. One of the latter's steam railmotors is on the right. (Lens of Sutton coll.)

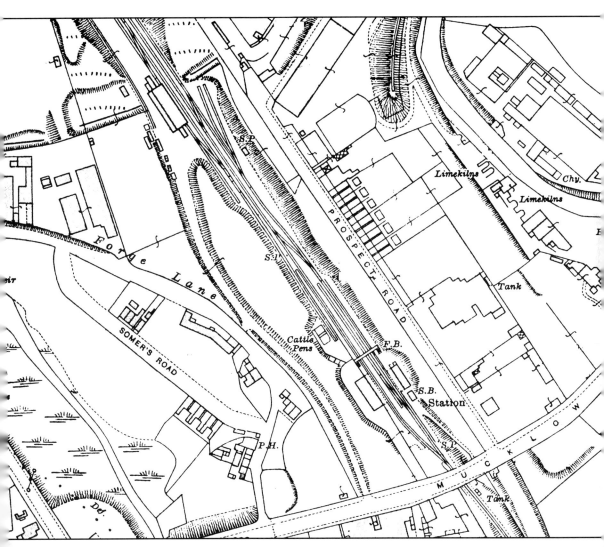

XI. This is a continuation of the previous extract and shows the main road passing over the single line to Longbridge at the bottom. From 1919, the highway was numbered A458. The 1938 records show a 6-ton crane here and a 12-ton one at the basin.

Gt Western Ry   Gt Western Ry
Windmill End   Windmill End
TO
OLD HILL HIGH STREET (Halt)
THIRD CLASS
1½d Fare 1½d
Issued subject to the conditions & regulations set
out in the Company's TimeTables, Bills & Notices
Old Hill (H.St.)   Old Hill (H.St)

4787   4787

53.   This location is immediately north of the station and is seen on 5th November 1947 as GWR
0-6-0PT no. 4696 shunts on the left and LMS 0-6-0 no. 22630 assembles a train for Longbridge on
the right. (Stephenson Locomotive Society coll.)

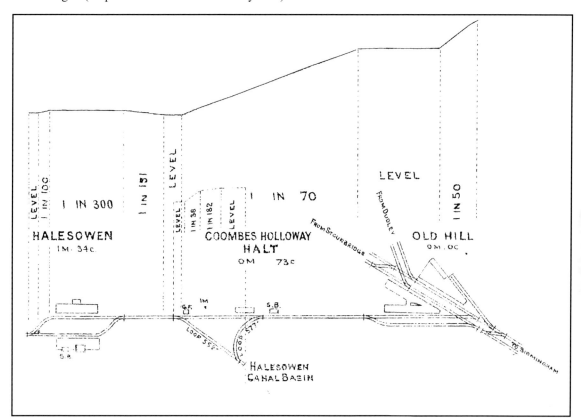

54.   The date is 30th May 1959 and 0-6-0 no. 58271 hauled the train between Old Hill and Halesowen. The term "up" was applied to trains running northwards and also southwards from this station. (H.C.Casserley)

55.   The footbridge had long gone, as public service had ceased in 1927. In the left distance is the goods shed, which was in use until the end. (Lens of Sutton coll.)

56.   Recorded on 18th September 1961 is 0-6-0PT no. 3658. The rails beyond the signal are dull, but those of the Longbridge route are bright. They were not used after 6th January 1964. (M.A.N.Johnston)

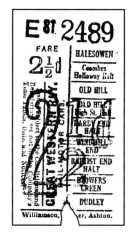

57.   Another 1961 photograph and this gives a fine panorama from the other end. It includes the goods shed and the row of electric lights, which were added in about 1960 to supplement the gas ones. (P.J.Kelley)

58.   Our final view is from 17th October 1963. Longbridge trains for workmen had called here regularly from 31st March 1928 until 1st September 1958. They had also run for a period from 1917. A new 25-lever frame had been installed in 1948. (R.G.Nelson/T.Walsh)

HUNNINGTON

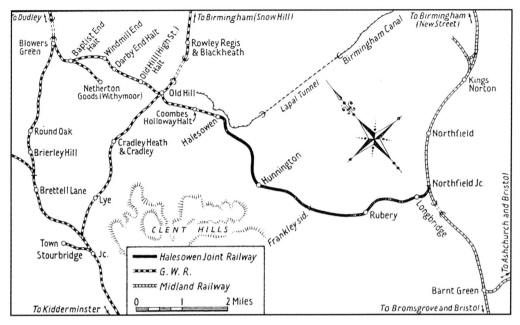

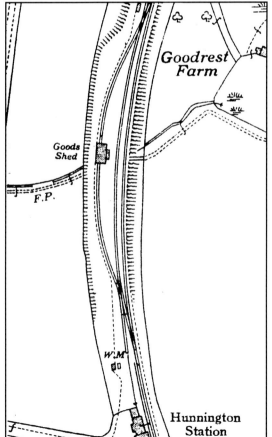

XII.   Map to show the pre-1923 owner-
ship. (Railway Magazine)

XIII.   The 1937 survey includes the goods
shed on a second loop; neither appeared on
the 1918 edition. There was a station master
here until October 1959.

↗ 59. Our   survey   comprises   two
photographs from 1950, when the platform
was only used by car factory workers. This
one includes the goods yard, which was in
use until the line closed in 1964.
(R.S.Carpenter)

→ 60. The station building was of a
standard MR design, as was the fencing.
It was occupied by railway staff, which
explains the tidy appearance. Traffic
included products of the Bluebell Toffee
Works. (P.B.Whitehouse)

61.   The most notable engineering feature on the route was Dowery Dell Viaduct, its nine spans being of lattice steel structure. Bound for Longbridge with Austin workers on 12th July 1939 is 0-6-0PT no. 2718. (H.C.Casserley)

62.   The viaduct was 234yds in length and had a severe weight restriction limiting locomotive sizes. The track was on a 1 in 50 gradient up from Halesowen and there was a 10mph speed limit on the bridge. (H.C.Casserley)

63.   South of the viaduct were Frankley Sidings and a typical workmens train is running past the ground frame on 29th May 1935. The 0-6-0PT is no. 1504 of the 1500 class of the GWR, which operated all such trains west of Longbridge. (H.C.Casserley)

64.   Recorded on 12th July 1939 was LMS 0-6-0 no. 22818. There were often as many as eight such trains in a day on this section of the route. (H.C.Casserley)

65.   Frankley Sidings were provided in about 1902 in connection with the construction of a reservoir and they were on the east side of the line. They were used subsequently for the conveyance of sand for the filter beds and are seen in 1947. They were removed in 1957. The water came from the Elan Valley in a 73-mile long pipe line. (R.S.Carpenter)

RUBERY

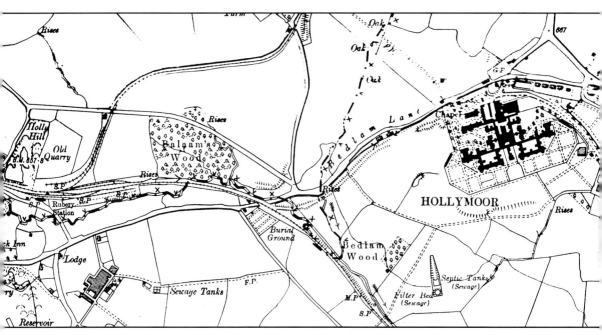

XIV.   The 1921 survey includes the earthworks for the short-lived branch to Hollymoor Hospital, used during its construction in 1901-05. Top left is the line to Birmingham Corporation's Bartley Reservoir, the sidings dating from about 1897.

66.   This is a view south from the quarry, which is marked on the left of the maps. The station building is left of centre. (Lens of Sutton coll.)

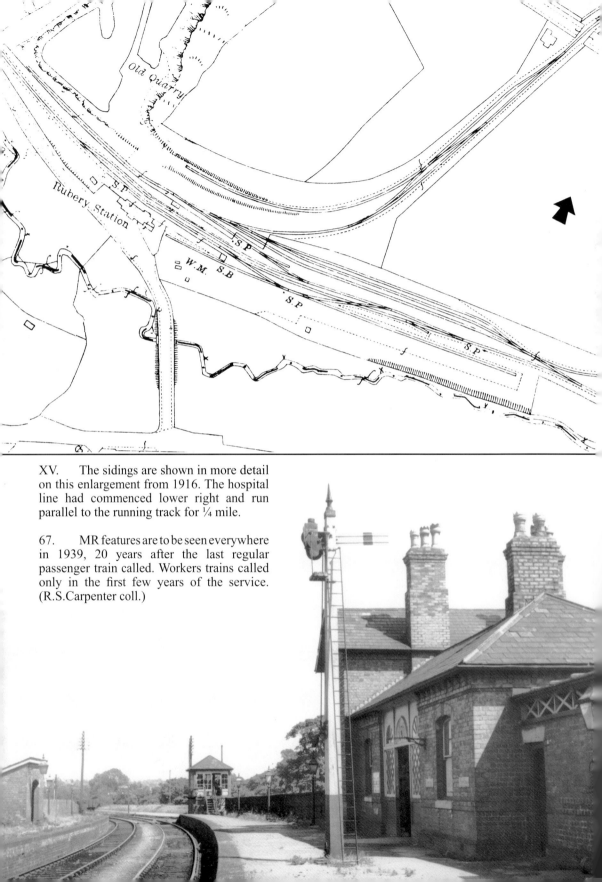

XV.   The sidings are shown in more detail on this enlargement from 1916. The hospital line had commenced lower right and run parallel to the running track for ¼ mile.

67.   MR features are to be seen everywhere in 1939, 20 years after the last regular passenger train called. Workers trains called only in the first few years of the service. (R.S.Carpenter coll.)

68.　　Ex-MR 0-6-0 no. 58126 approaches on 8th July 1950, with freight from Longbridge. The goods yard remained open until the line closed. The coal seems to have fallen off the back of a tender. (R.S.Carpenter coll.)

69.　　The SLS brought a rare sight of visitors on 2nd November 1963. Blowing off at the other end of the train is another 2-6-0, no. 46421. This was the last train to traverse the former MR section. (Stephenson Locomotive Society coll.)

LONGBRIDGE WORKS

XVI. This map overlaps no. XIV, but is from 1938 and shows the extent of the Austin car factory. It omits the station, which was near the word *Rea*. The Gloucester to Birmingham main line is on the right and there was a station on it, north of the road bridge, in 1841-49 and again from 1978.

➡ 70. The works was established in 1905 by Herbert Austin and the premises grew in 1910 when car production started. Massive extension took place for war production work and part of the factory is seen in 1921. The MR provided trains for workers to stations in the Birmingham area. (R.S.Carpenter coll.)

↘ 71. There was expansion vertically and laterally during World War II, the former being evident in this photograph from 13th April 1951. The train on the right has come from Old Hill behind 0-6-0PT no. 7428, while the other had left Saltley at 7.05am behind ex LMS 2-6-4T no. 72337. (T.J.Edgington)

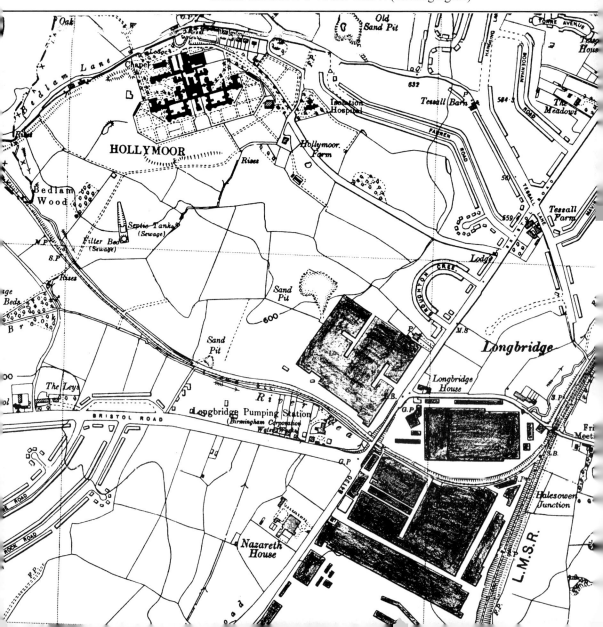

72.   West Box and part of Jubilee Sidings were recorded in July 1957. Austin and Morris had become part of the British Motor Corporation in 1952, but the names remained on the cars. British Leyland was its successor in 1968, this becoming the Rover Group in 1986 and eventually MG Rover Group. (H.C.Casserley)

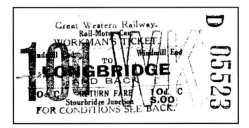

73.   The 5.09pm to Old Hill was hauled by no. 7432 on 8th July 1957. The Saltley service ceased in January 1960, just after Mini production started. This car was to become a legend, with over 5 million produced here in 41 years. (H.C.Casserley)

74.   The last car to be made here was a Rover 75 in June 2005 and all rail traffic ceased at that time. The conveyor connection over the Bristol Road was still standing in July 2006, as was the 1930s station building. It was used for parcels and ticket sales, but there was no public access to trains. (V.Mitchell)

HALESOWEN JUNCTION

75.   A MR 0-6-0 takes the Halesowen line with an engineers train in about 1905. The connection would later handle vast quantities of coal and materials inwards to the factory, with cars and scrap metal outwards. (M.Whitehouse coll.)

→ 76. Part of the Austin Works is in the background as a new signal box nears completion in 1929. It had a 65-lever frame and was fully functional until 1969. The Halesowen tracks can be seen behind the steps of the old box. (R.S.Carpenter coll.)

→ 77. Freight passes under the massive water main and is bound for Bristol behind 0-6-0 no. 44135, sometime in 1955-56. The present station was opened beyond the bridge on 8th May 1978. (R.S.Carpenter coll.)

Our *Bromsgrove to Birmingham* album
contains views of the factory sidings and
locomotives, together with the new station.

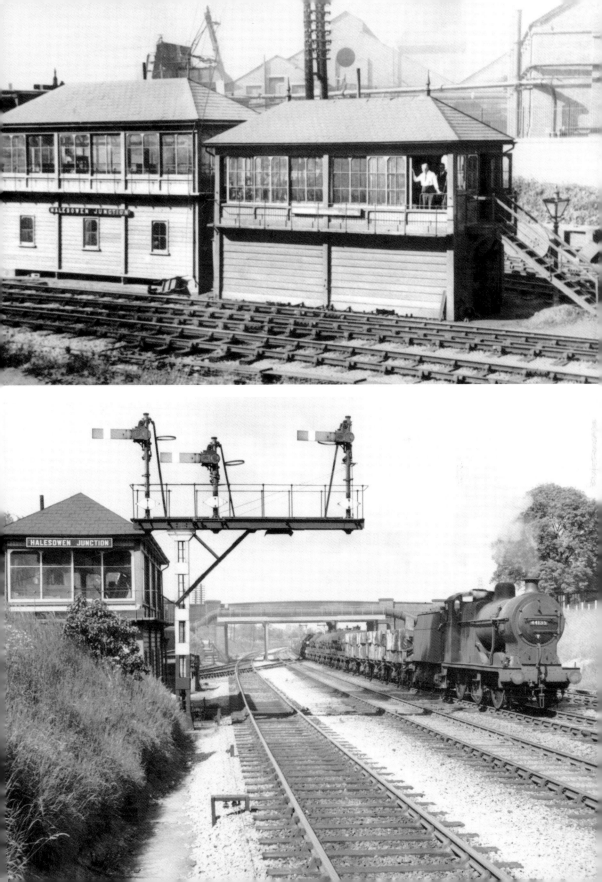

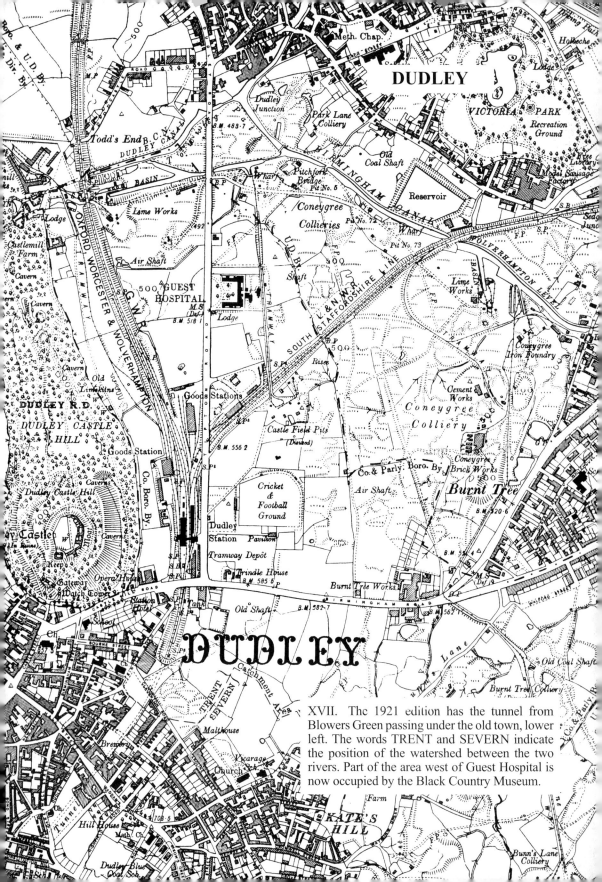

XVII. The 1921 edition has the tunnel from Blowers Green passing under the old town, lower left. The words TRENT and SEVERN indicate the position of the watershed between the two rivers. Part of the area west of Guest Hospital is now occupied by the Black Country Museum.

78.   A photograph from the south in the 1930s shows autocoach no. 45 in the bay on the GWR side of the station. The LMS entrance is top right. (Lens of Sutton coll.)

79.   Standing at the same platform in about 1938 is railcar no. 8, which was built in 1936 and seated 70 people. South signal box is on the left. (Lens of Sutton coll.)

80.   We can now enjoy two photographs of steam on 24th March 1951. Ex-LMS 2-6-2T no. 41226 waits at the ex-LNWR platform, while one of their 0-8-0s stands in the background. The train is the push-pull service to Dudley Port. (B.W.L.Brooksbank)

81.   Ex-GWR 2-6-2T no. 4101 approaches the island platform with a Wolverhampton Low Level to Worcester Shrub Hill service. In the distance is North box, which had 27 levers. (B.W.L.Brooksbank)

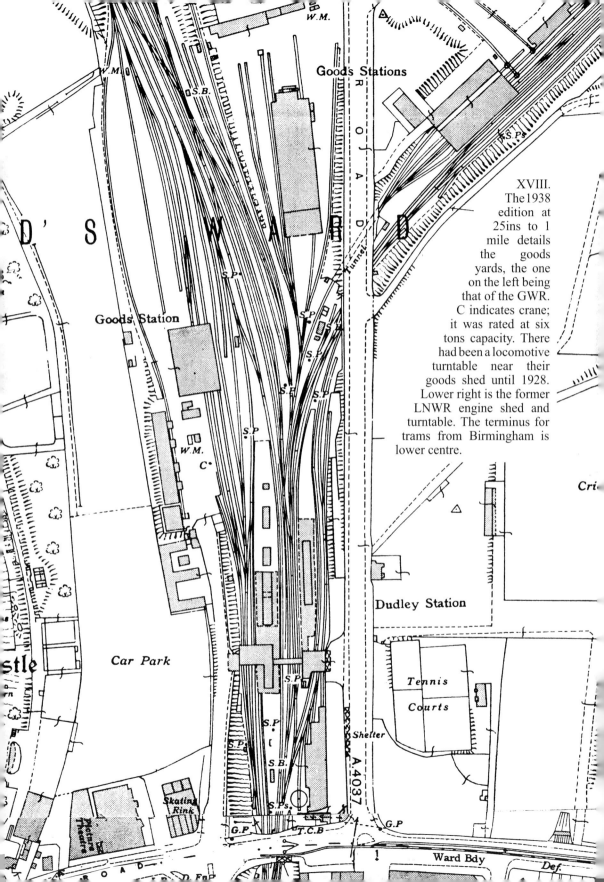

Goods Stations

W.M.

S.B.

S.Ps

D'S WARD

Goods Station

S.P

S.P

S.P

S.P.

S.P.

S.P

S.P.

W.M.

C

XVIII.
The 1938 edition at 25ins to 1 mile details the goods yards, the one on the left being that of the GWR. C indicates crane; it was rated at six tons capacity. There had been a locomotive turntable near their goods shed until 1928. Lower right is the former LNWR engine shed and turntable. The terminus for trams from Birmingham is lower centre.

Cri

Dudley Station

Car Park

stle

S.P

Tennis

Courts

S.P

S.P.

Shelter

S.B.

A.4037

Skating Rink

S.Ps

G.P

T.C.B

G.P

Ward Bdy

Def

ROAD

82. A panorama from about 1955 includes 0-6-0PT no. 8742 simmering at the stops of platform 3. The left side of the station was designated "Castle" on 19th July 1950 and the right became "Town". (R.S.Carpenter)

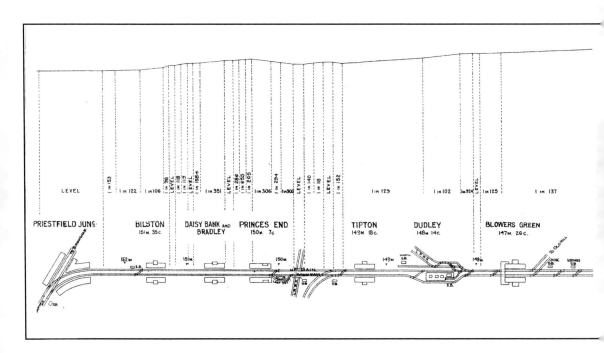

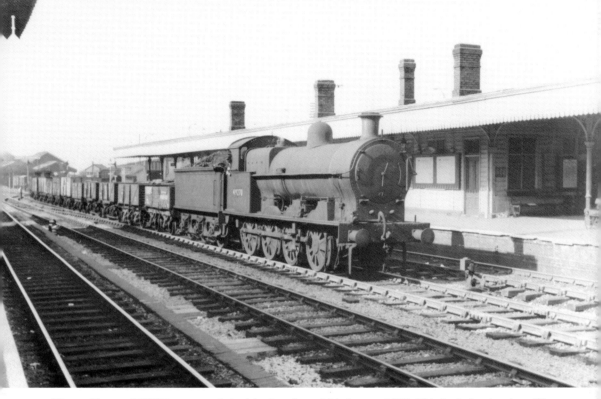

83.   Former LNWR property is in this view from 14th August 1956. This includes the class G2a 0-8-0. The goods shed in the background was the GWR bonded warehouse. (D.A.Johnson)

84.   Recorded on the same day at the ex-GWR platform is no. 7005 *Lamphey Castle* with the 8.25pm Wolverhampton Low Level to Worcester Shrub Hill. The train called at all stations, except two. (D.A.Johnson)

85.　　Steam obscures much of the station as ex-LNER class B1 4-6-0 no. 61006 *Blackbuck* departs to Lincoln, with a return Dudley Zoo excursion. This view is from the Tipton Road on 2nd April 1961. General goods traffic ceased on 6th July 1964, as did the final passenger service (from Old Hill). Parcel traffic continued here until the end of 1966. (T.J.Edgington)

→ 86. A panorama from 12th October 1961 reveals that some repairs have been done to the Town side, which was actually furthest from the town. The GWR had a staff of 33 here in 1929, with a further 20 in their goods depot. (R.G.Nelson/T.Walsh)

→ 87. This photograph records the arrival of the last train from Old Hill; it was hauled by 0-6-0PT no. 7418 and the date was 13th June 1964. South box closed on 16th July 1967. It had a new 71-lever frame in 1935. (G.Sidwell)

88.	The north end of the island platform once used by GWR trains was photographed on 13th June 1964, as 2-6-2T no. 4555 stood with a SLS railtour. The loco was preserved and has run on the Paignton & Dartmouth Railway for many years.
(Stephenson Locomotive Society coll.)

➔ 89. Nos 9610 and 9630 arrived on 11th September 1966, more than two years after the last scheduled passenger train. "The Farewell to the 0-6-0PTs" started at Snow Hill; the tour included Halesowen, Snow Hill and Stratford-upon-Avon.
(G.Adams/M.J.Stretton coll.)

➔ 90.	The site was cleared of buildings and a Freightliner Terminal opened there on 6th November 1967. It was in use until 29th September 1986. This northward view has the 1967 55-lever signal box and the line to Wednesbury on the right. The photograph is from the early 1980s. No. 40012 has just reversed the containers under the gantry. (B.Robbins)

TIPTON FIVE WAYS

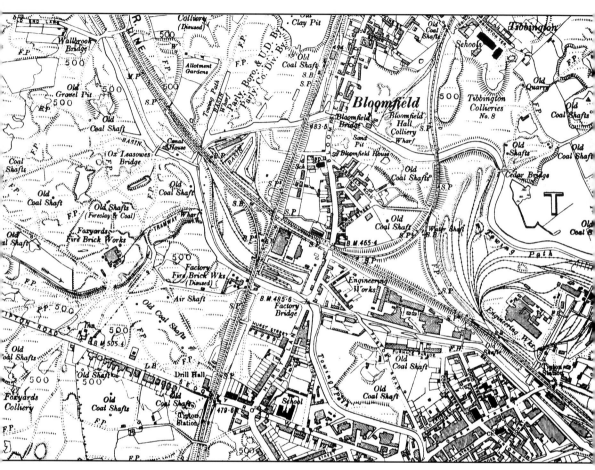

XIX.   Our route is almost vertical, with the station near the lower border of this 1921 extract. The LNWR's main line is diagonal and the tracks north from the triangle lead to Wednesbury Town. The curve from the GWR to the LNWR had opened when the line was extended north from Dudley. The OWWR's own line to Wolverhampton (Low Level) opened for passenger trains on 1st July 1854 and the curve was disconnected at its north end in 1860. The sidings south of the curve to the canal basin were GWR property, but in February 1958 they were transferred from the WR to the LMR. When the ex-GWR route closed, the connection to the former LNWR line was restored to maintain access to the sidings at the basin. Most collieries in this area closed in 1919.

91. The station opened with the line, but was not provided with a goods yard. The complex of sidings shown on the map near the canal basin was LNWR property. We look towards the south in 1950. The suffix "Five Ways" was added on 19th July 1950. The name was also applied to the sidings from that time. (Stations UK)

92. A view northwards in 1963 includes the bridge over Sedgley Road and part of the former coalfield. Passenger service had been withdrawn on 30th July 1962, but the line was used for freight until 1968. (P.J.Garland/R.S.Carpenter coll.)

PRINCES END
& COSELEY

XX.   This map continues from the top of the previous one. Please turn back to this, as the small goods yard is on it, near Bloomfield. The longest siding terminates at a small canal basin on the Birmingham Canal.

➜ 93. The station opened in December 1856 and the suffix was added in January 1936. A local train from Dudley is seen behind 2-6-2T no. 6132, shortly before closure. (Stephenson Locomotive Society coll.)

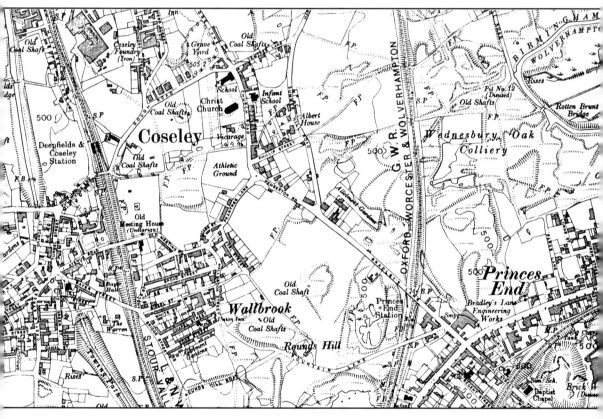

➜ 94. A year later and we can see the connection to the goods yard, which was in use until 30th January 1968, when the route closed. (P.J.Garland/R.S.Carpenter coll.)

DAISY BANK & BRADLEY

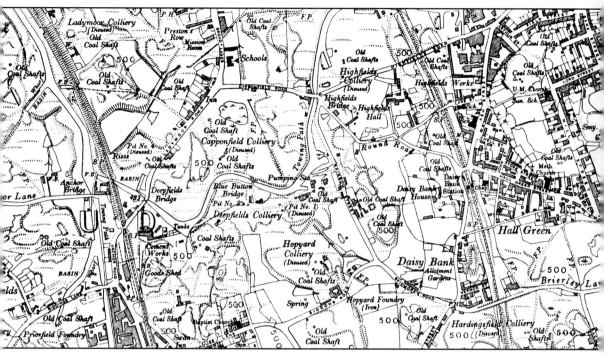

XXI. This 1921 extract also continues from the previous one, with our route on the right. This station opened with the line in 1854.

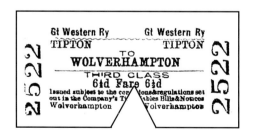

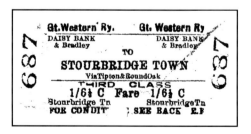

95.   Two photographs from 1963 indicate the situation only months after final closure to passengers. It had closed from 1st January 1917 until 3rd February 1919, due to staff shortage. There were two men here subsequently. (R.G.Nelson/T.Walsh)

96.   A view south includes a colliery tip and generous space allowed for broad gauge track, which was probably never completed this far north.The suffix was applied in 1919. (P.J.Garland/R.S.Carpenter coll.)

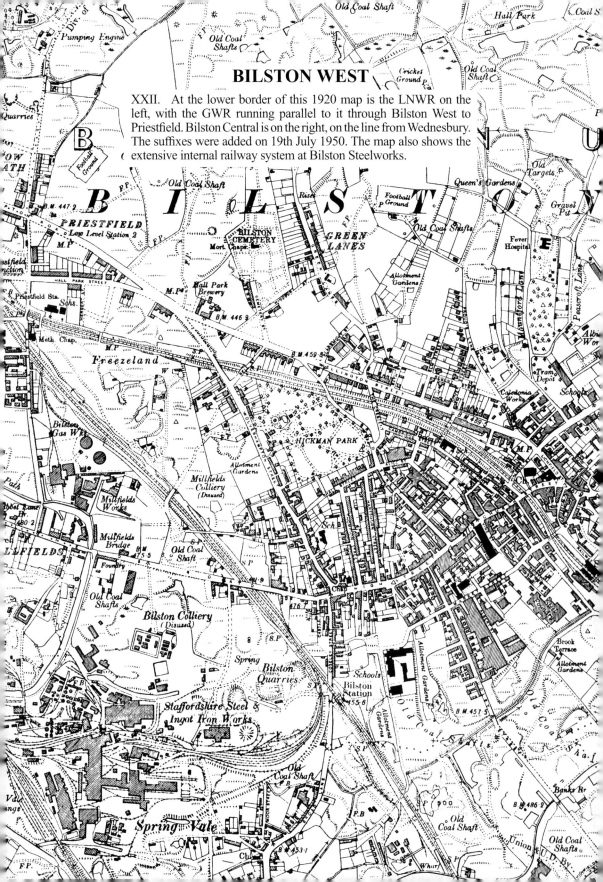

BILSTON WEST

XXII. At the lower border of this 1920 map is the LNWR on the left, with the GWR running parallel to it through Bilston West to Priestfield. Bilston Central is on the right, on the line from Wednesbury. The suffixes were added on 19th July 1950. The map also shows the extensive internal railway system at Bilston Steelworks.

97.   All the three photographs are from 1963. First, we look north and see Bilston West box (1878-1968) in the distance, together with the connection to Hickmans Branch. This was the official name long after Alfred Hickman's Spring Vale Ironworks from the 1880s became Stewart & Lloyds' property in 1925. (R.G.Nelson/T.Walsh)

98.   Moving north, we look from the footbridge at the branch junction and see part of the West Midland Gas Board's Bilston Gasworks in the distance. Their sidings are on the left of the map. (P.J.Garland/R.S.Carpenter coll.)

99.   This panorama was recorded from the bridge in the background of the previous picture. The station footbridge is in the distant haze. On the right is another S&L siding. (R.G.Nelson/T.Walsh)

1851

2nd-SINGLE SINGLE-2nd

Daisy Bank & Bradley to

Daisy Bank & B'ley Daisy Bank & B'ley
Priestfield   Priestfield

PRIESTFIELD

(W)   6d. Fare 6d.   (W)

For conditions see over For conditions see over

1851

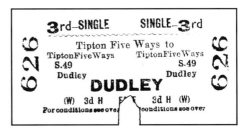

626

3rd-SINGLE   SINGLE-3rd

Tipton Five Ways to

TiptonFiveWays   TiptonFiveWays
S.49   S.49
Dudley   Dudley

DUDLEY

(W)   3d H   3d H   (W)

For conditions see over   conditions see over

626

Priestfield
Junction   Old
              Coal Shaft

S.P.

S.P.

Priestfield
Station

F.B.

F.P.

P.H.

F.P.

S.P.

HALL   PARK   STREET

PRIESTFIELD

XXIII. The junction area is seen
in 1919 at 25ins to 1 mile. The
gasworks sidings are included. The
route top right is from Wednesbury
and it is currently used by the
Midland Metro.

FREEZELAND STREET

PRIESTFIELD ST.

S.P.

S.B.

t Ground

AGE   Bowling
             Green

Methodist Chapel
(Primitive)

Fre

S.P.

F.P.

FLEECE STREET

OXFORD, WORCESTER & WOLVERHAMPTON

G.W.R.

VICTORIA TERRACE

P.H.

F.P.

Well

MARS STREET

OAK STREET

C.B.

WARD STREET

Div. of Parly. Boro. Bdy.

C.B.

Tk.

Tk.

ath

Tks.

Tk.

Tk.

Gas Works
(Bilston Gas Light & Co

100.   The Wednesbury route to Birmingham is on the left and is seen from a train from Dudley on 13th August 1955. (R.M.Casserley)

101.   Working the 4.48pm Wolverhampton to Worcester on 1st June 1957 is no. 6828 *Trellech Grange*. (T.J.Edgington)

102.   No doubt much locally produced steel was used in the construction of the footbridge, as well as the gas holder. (P.J.Garland/R.S.Carpenter coll.)

103.   Beyond the 36-lever signal box is the end of a line which formed a loop half a mile in length. Stow Heath box was near the other end of it. The box had a 48-lever frame and closed on 19th June 1968, as did Priestfield. (P.J.Garland/R.S.Carpenter coll.)

PASSENGERS
ARE NOT ALLOWED TO
CROSS the RAILWAY
EXCEPT BY MEANS OF
THE BRIDGE

104. The charming waiting room, complete with brick chimney, is worthy of close examination. Staffing ceased on 5th May 1968 and so there would be no more cosy fires. (P.J.Garland/R.S.Carpenter coll.)

105. The last of four photographs from 1963 completes our survey. The two platforms in the background were in use until 6th March 1972. (P.J.Garland/R.S.Carpenter coll.)

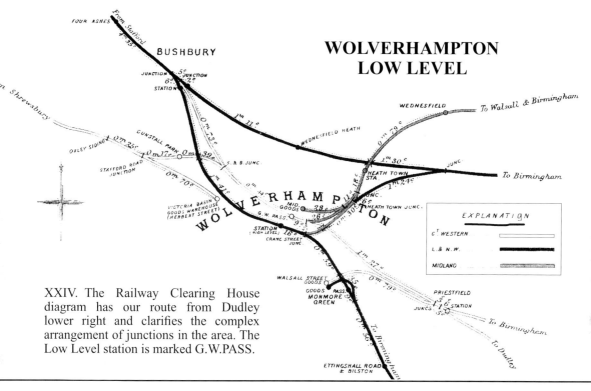

WOLVERHAMPTON
LOW LEVEL

EXPLANATION

G^T WESTERN	
L. & N.W.	
MIDLAND	

XXIV. The Railway Clearing House diagram has our route from Dudley lower right and clarifies the complex arrangement of junctions in the area. The Low Level station is marked G.W.PASS.

106.   A picture from about 1900 includes 4-4-0 no. 3310 *St. Just* and 0-4-2T no. 550, which was in use from 1869 to 1929. This is the north end in about 1920. The overall roof was removed between October 1933 and May 1934 without interfering with the station's work. (HMRS)

107.   A view south on 18th June 1952 features ex-LMS class 2P 4-4-0 no. 40501 standing at the down platform with an engineers saloon. It has run via the ex-LMS line through Wednesfield. (Stephenson Locomotive Society coll.)

108.   Standing near South Box is 0-6-0PT no. 9658. The railway observers, above the cab, are near the dock line near which there was once a wagon turntable serving sidings to the buildings behind. (D.K.Jones coll.)

109.   This is the west facade in about 1950, with the elevated lines of the High Level station in the background. (Stephenson Locomotive Society coll.)

110.   North Box is in the background and the goods lines are on the right in this view from the 1960s. (Lens of Sutton coll.)

111.	We are at the east end after the removal of the scissors crossovers between the up tracks in 1964. On the left is one of the docks used for parcels traffic. (Lens of Sutton coll.)

112.	The curve at the west end was an undesirable feature operationally. The sheds on the left were used for carriage storage and had connections to the main line at both ends. The high wall once supported the roof. (Lens of Sutton coll.)

113. These two backing signals survived near South box until about 1962. In the distance is the smoky Wolverhampton Tunnel, 377yds in length. The MR tracks were laid above it. South box closed on 23rd May 1973; it had 97 levers. (P.C.Coutanche)

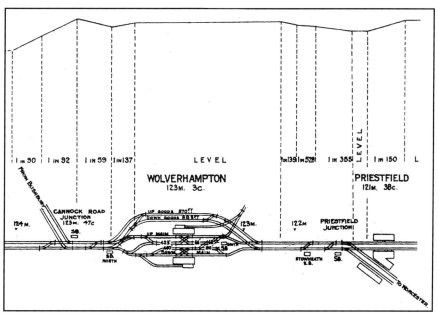

114.   This is the train described in caption 89 and much photographed on its complex journey. (G.Adams/M.J.Stretton coll.)

115.   The date is 4th March 1967 for this and the next two photographs. No. 4079 *Pendennis Castle* heads the Ian Allan "Birkenhead Flyer". (Stephenson Locomotive Society coll.)

116.   No. D3027 is at the High Level station while no. D1605 waits to depart north. Through services would cease that day. (M.J.Stretton)

117.   No. D1601 is arriving with an up train, while a DMU waits to leave from the down platform. (M.J.Stretton)

118.   The west end was recorded in 1968, with the electrified tracks of the High Level station on the right. Through passenger services were withdrawn on 6th March 1967 and the final local services followed on 6th March 1972. The bays on the right were once used for Wellington and Wombourn trains. (Stations UK)

119.   Only the east end of the down platform was used by the final passenger trains and access to it was by a walkway over the dock trackbed. Parcel traffic was concentrated here and no. 08782 was recorded amongst the vans in January 1979. There is catenary in the background. (S.Davey)

120.   The station was used as a parcel depot until 1st June 1981 and this was the scene at the east end in 2003. Dereliction continued until 2006, when redevelopment for business and residential purposes began and restoration of these structures took place. (M.Dart)

MP Middleton Press

EVOLVING THE ULTIMATE RAIL ENCYCLOPEDIA

Easebourne Lane, Midhurst, West Sussex.
GU29 9AZ   Tel:01730 813169

www.middletonpress.co.uk   email:info@middletonpress.co.uk
A-978 0 906520   B- 978 1 873793   C- 978 1 901706   D-978 1 904474   E - 978 1 906008

OOP Out of print at time of printing - Please check availability   BROCHURE AVAILABLE SHOWING NEW TITLES